ALSO BY EMILY PERKOVICH

*Expulsion*
*Godshots Wanted: Apply Within*
*Swallow*
*baby, sweetheart, honey*
*Manipulate Me, Babe—I Trust You*

# The Number 12 Looks
# Just Like You

*poems by*

# Emily Perkovich

*Finishing Line Press*
Georgetown, Kentucky

# The Number 12 Looks Just Like You

## ACKNOWLEDGMENTS

"When Ana Was Born" & "Spring Cleaning" first appeared in *Godshots Wanted: Apply Within*

"I learned today that Bridget Jones was trying to lose 20lbs because she weighed 135" first appeared in *baby, sweetheart, honey*

"the body prepares for a riot" first appeared in *Rogue Agent* – Issue 98

"Stress Eating & Starving" was reworked for this collection but has previously appeared as a micro-piece on *The Prose*

Publisher: Leah Huete de Maines
Editor: Christen Kincaid
Cover Art: Emily Perkovich
Author Photo: Emily Perkovich
Cover Design: Elizabeth Maines McCleavy

Order online: www.finishinglinepress.com
also available on amazon.com

Author inquiries and mail orders:
Finishing Line Press
PO Box 1626
Georgetown, Kentucky 40324
USA

# Table of Contents

# Introduction

I had initially written something very different for the beginning of this book. I wanted to point out all of the reasons why I talk so much about my eating disorder and body dysmorphia. While I was writing that, I got lost trying to explain a thought that we don't talk about enough.

People don't talk about mental health in healthy ways. The discomfort surrounding mental health topics is understandable because so many people do not believe in their existence at all. This all becomes so cyclical that it's impossible to tell what the actual issue is anymore—you don't believe me when I talk about my mental health, so I become unsure of myself when talking about my mental health, and then because I try to become palatable and agreeable, you further disregard that there was ever a problem to begin with. It's likely, in this environment, that we stop talking about the topic that is plaguing us constantly to avoid the discomfort.

The major problem with not talking about it is that no one is learning either. We aren't learning healthier more confident ways to talk about mental health, so non-believers continue to not understand and that breeds ignorance.

It's not fair, but if we want change, it's the people suffering already, that are going to have to push their own boundaries and learn to teach, learn to make people listen.

More than any other audience, I want people that don't relate to this book to read more work like this. I want you to look and say, "holy shit, I can't imagine that, but I want to know what to look for in others because it seems inhumane to suffer through that alone." I want people that don't believe in mental health to not look and say, "she's pretty and skinny. Why is she obsessing over her body?" Or "well she could just listen to the people around her and start eating and stop thinking about it!" But instead say, "wow, the crossover of mental health into physical health is amazing. The brain is so limitless. I wish her brain would let her see herself the way that I do! How can I help people going through this?"

I don't feel comfortable saying that I am 135lbs (many people's goal weight), and I look in the mirror and hate my body and get online and love so many other bodies—bigger and smaller than mine. I don't feel comfortable saying that I have thrown up in disgusting places in a moment of panic to control my body and what gets to stay with it. Or how many meals I have skipped. Or how often my body does not feel like a body. Or like it belongs to me. Or how I feel like parts of me are floating away. That sometimes, I romanticize the illness to cope with the illness. Or explaining things that have caused me to relapse. Or bringing up how many times I have pushed through recovery. I definitely don't feel comfortable in our supposed body positive culture saying I want my body to be smaller, even when I see larger bodies that I like infinitely more than my own. I don't feel comfortable trying to explain that mental health can be a social product while simultaneously being internal and something that is not going to disappear entirely by eliminating the obvious sources. I'm not comfortable with any of this. But I'm also not comfortable in my own skin, and I don't want this cycle to continue.

*This collection centers on eating disorders and body dysmorphia. There are also allusions to other forms of self-harm as well as domestic violence, generational and patriarchal trauma

Emily Perkovich—March 2022

## When Ana Was Born

You are raw egg hands. You are raw chicken hands. You are bruised-brows, bitten-tongues, locked-doors, bathtub-hiding, bloodied-knuckles hands. You are smoothing, tucking, tidying. You are garden-sheared hands clipping yourself into a more enviable skeleton. You are hair-curled, waist-slim, electric-skinned in shadows and lace. You are hairspray and bleach and ocean-eyeshadow over seaweed-irises. And that must be why I was born drowning in your eyes. I am measuring myself against the way I would fit too snug if you swallowed me whole. I am all olive and curves. I roll across myself in hills instead of waves while you flow into hipbone-tributaries and ribcage-levies. But erosion is inherited, so when my stomach growls, I remember how I was born from a siren, all dressed in divinity, and I let my canyon-echoes ring. They sing themselves into fetal-void. Me, all pregnant with starvation. And your knobby knees knelt in the dirt of me, planting the seeds, but the moment of conception came from violence. It was my face pressed deep into dinner-plate mess. And I keep trying to piece together the labor and delivery. I keep looking for the moment the aversion to sustenance crowned. Was it the way your cheekbones cradled your thin smile? The way your ethereal hands shushed and hushed post-destruction? I can't be sure. But I remember the way my hair hung limp, brushing my too-buried collar bones, greased with fried-chicken skin. My nose bled out mashed potatoes and gravy as after-birth. And you handed me silence, so I named her famine.

## Call Me Abstract

walk through the dizzy spells, walk through the dizzy spells,
                                     walk through the dizzy spells,

Know you are the places where you ache

Call these the magic words for failing
For fainting
See here, where the light can't find the shape

This is how the breaking turns muddy, turns circles, turns out,
                                     turns the phrase,

the sounds are left dizzy, talk through the dizzy spells

There is no clarity in the places where you ache

You bottle the breath from the lamb because the slaughter came
quick, there is too much blood in this breath, turns the stomach,
turns foul, turns to retch,

Your blood is toxic when stored incorrectly

Your stomach is not a vessel

There is a downward motion to the way the spiral has learned to mix

And you,

fall through the dizzy spells, fall through the dizzy spells,
                                     fall through the fall and fall and fall

## How to Become a Micro Poem

I'm an expert at drowning.
And I've lost six pounds this week
"Was it healthy?"
My mouth tongues at the silence
"Are you eating?"
And I can hold my breath forever.

**I learned today that Bridget Jones was trying to lose 20lbs because she weighed 135**

I fell in love with a skeleton smile when I learned my midriff would show in my new cheer uniform, you show off your waist once, and the world never lets you go back into hiding.
There is always the comparison
Say, this many less
This many less
This many less
This many less
Please. Please, say less, less, less
My navel was a part of my mother and my navel causes me trauma
My mother's navel has also caused her trauma
And my mother's mother
My grandma's navel was a part of many other navels before it was traumatic
My grandma can only eat certain foods
My grandma stayed in hospitals
My grandma destroyed a few organs
My grandma almost disappeared
My grandma says don't let your navel cause trauma
And my navel still likes to cause me trauma, because once you show your waist, the world never lets you go back into hiding.
I try to kiss the plate, but my navel isn't mine, and it's stuck in a time loop betraying us all, and I think how the only time I ever really prayed was before I put on my uniform or after I ate, and how those weren't the same types of praying, and how neither of those ended in belief
I think, less, less, please
Less.

## The body prepares for a riot

I eat my inner child but only for protection, tie a daisy chain around each finger, I will not lose myself again, but I am swelling around the ribs

I am unsure where to find myself behind all of this skin

It's like the way I have chosen to sweat myself out when I used to focus on kneeling, no, I never kneeled in rice, no, I never held a firework in my mouth, no, I never held my hand to a stovetop, but I knelt in my insides, I held my insides in my mouth, I held my hand to my insides,

The purpose of the exercise is to stop the swelling, the purpose of the exercise has been found to end in breaking, inflammation, scarring, the purpose of the exercise is to remind myself that the insides look as bad as the outside, but no one ever wanted to save the marrow from being tender

I become crescent, worship myself waning, refuse to wax waxing, never become the becoming

My body becomes the riot

## clean the plate

ok, let's start here, let's remember it's just a few more bites, let's remember that the scraps are wasteful, no one asked if you were hungry, i don't care if you like it, you eat what i give you, your mother works all day, your mother slaved over this meal, your mother only eats the left overs, and we're not leaving left overs, i said you eat what i give you, remember it's wasteful, don't make me come over there, i said i don't care if you like it, i want you to eat it, if you don't finish that, i'm going to show you how to finish that, if you cry, i'm going to give you something to cry about, look what you made me do, don't you dare gag, i swear if you fucking throw up, why can't you just listen, why can't you just eat what i give you, you have no respect for your mother, you're so wasteful, you made a fucking mess, clean up the floor, wash your face

**confession in which i become dizzy so many times a day that i wonder if gravity is out to get me**

i want to look like that i want to look like that i want to look like that there's something about it the way his bones stick out and i want to look like that the way his ribs are reaching out to me

reward – (n.)
/rə'wôrd/

- a stimulus given in return for a desired response
- we can block the binge
- skeletons whisper sweet nothings, but you have to have thin-skin to hear, you'll want to reduce the layers, flay the obstructions away, melt away the thick spots, burn out the detritus
- this is a cleansing by fire

i'm on my knees meditating on the word convenient

or

i'm on my knees and i'm thinking of the convenience in the fact that more water helps the carbs go down and more water helps the carbs come back up

punishment – (n.)
/'pənishmənt/

- a penalty inflicted or imposed as retribution
- no one knows how to lie quite the way the mirror does
- no one knows how to lie like the punishment disguised as the reward

most illness tends to present as duality rather than antithesis

that's called catch 22, that's called vicious circle, call it ouroboros, and you can see the way that it's a punishment for the reward for the punishment for the way that the reward in the illness is in the punishment

**Purge**

It's a shipwreck, or it's blood, or it's meat
It's not insides
It's not meant for insides
You can tell by the way it crashes, the way it pulls, the way it aches to
thrash at the edge of the waves
Wants to drown in the acid flood
Does the debris always froth this way? Always clot this way? Stick,
stink, sting this way?
It demands letting
But whoever asked anyone to hold an onslaught in their wake?
Funerals for the drowned are only funerals for the lost, only funerals
for the missing, really, only funerals for the ones missing the lost
And no one ever missed a shipwreck, missed the blood,
                                                    missed the meat

## dissipate

My mouth is eating me alive. Letting my insides melt away until I'm all sharp edges. It's like a balancing act I never perfect. Because the lesser part of me feels more when I neglect my plate. When my scale slowly dips digit by digit. When the clothes start to bunch and hang a bit loose at the seams. It's like a tightrope, but I always lose. Because the disappearing side has less to hold up. And the side that's filling itself full, all goes crashing. It's like the weight is pulling me into the ground. Burying me, still breathing. So I empty into earthquakes. Shake, rattle, roll. Let my insides reverberate as canyon-echo tremor. And it's like the dirt falls away with each churning shudder. Aching and stained. And I finally float.

## This and smaller

There is an intrinsic link between the trauma response and the wish to be less apparent, to disappear, to haunt the space rather than take up the space

It's apparent that I am too heavy based on the space I take up in my own head

I'm taking up space, and that feels heavy, leaves me haunted, I've been doing my best not to idle over the things that hurt, but old habits die hard and this tearing open wounds is an addiction, and if I'm empty there's only space

It's the seconds in between that house the hurt, the emptying that turns into a haunting

There's a spinning here, a cyclone, I mean cycle, it's a circle, it's a haunting, it's control by becoming the haunting, what I'm saying is all this control is too controlling, I take over control, and now I become apparent, and I control that by disappearing

What I'm saying is, I can only crawl so far into myself because there's no room left for myself in here, and I empty, and I haunt, and it's a cycle, and the trauma gains control, the trauma takes control

# Whelm

I have always weighed myself. Sometimes in pain and ache. Occasionally in an inundating lust for loss. But most often in disgust. Today I saw the scales tip in favor of a tidy 30 pounds of abhorrence. And I think of how just 30 pounds back I still weighed at least 10 too many. And before that it may have been 5 and occasionally 10 but it has never been a thin, slim zero. The integers have never been positive in my favor. I am negative in self-worth. I am fractions, overwhelmed. 5s over 3s. I am the space that I fill, and it has always been too much, though I am still somehow never quite enough. And I sometimes wonder if that is because I have left my more worthy pieces drowning in porcelain pools and occasionally scattered across untouched plates. I have clawed to the back of my throat searching for the gods that might dwell there, and I have always come up short, retching out demons and hail and plagues. My mouth pours only self-taught lies and acid suicides. And my stomach often growls. Discontent turning of aching hell hounds, attention-starved. And I am scratching the sky for wishing-stars, wanting for hands that might be large enough to hold me so that when I compare them to the mirror, I seem to disappear in contrast. But I only ever find the hands that leave me littered in violence. The ones that welt red and blossom indigo and violet. My skin, constellations with velvet bruises as the always-too-heavy backdrop. More visible than ever. My mind, raw meat. And all of me too little to fill up anyone but myself, all overfilled, too much.

Until I spew it from my pits. And the next time my nails touch the wet cave of my mouth, in search of reoccurring dreams, I hope that they whisper a prayer to that devil inside. Come forth and swallow me whole. Let me ache inside you, for once. Me as null. Me as void. Me, disappearing. Me, disappeared. Swallow me whole. Swallow me whole.

## Spring Cleaning

Hands reach to back of cabinet
Close on darkness
Close on shadows
The only thing that stays are shadows
How they hang against the body
How they open wide like the mouth
Like swallowing
And,
O, the swallowing!
Darken the doorway
This skeleton shape in sharpened fractures
The cabinet is just another mouth
This cabinet is starving
For affection
For calories
The only thing that stays are the calories
How they hang against the body
How the teeth clench against them
These calories like shadows in the mouth
How they come back to haunt
Ghosts of Dinners' Past
This cabinet is just another throat
Hands reach to back of throat
Push at wet
Push at flesh
The only thing that stays are the fingers
How they play in the purge
How they love the feel of an exorcism
And,
O, the fingers!
O, the calories!

## Stress Eating & Starving

I reach out and palm the antithesis, tip chin skyward, let it crawl
down my throat
I become empty vessel, swear off the urge to eat
Bones rattle in fear, terrified of anything but skin clutching their
framework
I starve, I starve, I starve
A vacant map of carefully crafted dysmorphia, I'm spoon-feeding my
wanting with self-taught lies
I starve, I starve, I
I become bursting body, filled, swear I am built to feast
Stomach swells, insides beg to fill, fill, fill
I am a rib cage fighting to contain the craving to binge and explode
I grow into both, I become empty vessel, I become bursting body,
neither is healthy, I am the binge and purge, I am the starving, neither
is sure of itself
I struggle, I control, I empty, I burst, but neither becomes a whole

## A List of Things No One Has Noticed

You realize there might be a problem, when your stomach quiets, it's been 6 days, it's been one cup of green beans, one half cup of rice, 12 x 6 cups of black coffee (and that's the measurement not the object), 4 - 24 oz vanilla iced coffees, one apple, one forced pancake (purged), 5 fries (chewed then spit into the trash), one cup of sugar-free strawberry jello (not the measurement, just the container), two spoonfuls of chicken broth, water estimated at around 6-7 gallons, sleep estimated at 20 hours

Day 3 became a cloud, you realize on day 6 that this is more than overcast, the forecast is dismal

Day 6 says you aren't hungry, day 6 says you aren't tired, day 6 says the coffee feels alive, the coffee is a buzzing, you are so alive, you are buzzing, day 6 says don't even try rice again, it won't stay down, day 6 says drink your water

## Joaquin Phoenix

I'm in a theater watching a man break for the cameras

I'm watching multiple mental illnesses turn his brain to a playground carousel because it's the only way some people can see that something is wrong with humanity

I stopped counting calories months ago

I'm watching grease paint and cigarettes
And everyone is watching the fancy foot work
And I'm watching the kinks in society
And I'm watching how many shadows in this room will walk out and not understand the message

And I'm watching

But, I'm watching the way his skin stretches when he breathes
I'm watching the marigold tint under his eyes
I'm watching his ribs, breaking like waves, stabbing, stabbing, stabbing, stabbing
I'm watching his ribs

And I cover my mouth because now my throat is closing and it feels so dry in here and my foot taps and I run my thumbs under my eyes and I'm not breathing because he is so fucking beautiful and I'm squeezing my clavicles but I haven't counted calories in months and there is too much there to grab on to and I haven't counted calories in months so now I'm kneeling in a fucking public restroom and I'm pressing two fingers in the center of my tongue in the center of my throat and the popcorn scratches my insides and the kernels float and the syrup sinks and I haven't counted calories in months so now I'm counting how much is in the water and is it less than what I ate because even a good purge will only help with about 50% of the binge and some sources say only 20% and I barely even drank any water so that can't be everything but I barely drank any water so now I'm resigned and I'm staring in that awful fluorescent lit mirror and I look tired but I don't look any smaller and I haven't counted calories in months but I'm resigned and I blow my nose and I swish tap water across my teeth and the woman behind me knows because she's staring and I don't really care because I probably just got some fucking disease from the dirty ass tile so why the hell should her opinion matter besides I haven't even counted calories in months so who is she to judge one moment of weakness and it's not like I have been counting calories I just didn't feel well

I return to my seat, my eyes water, I watch the man on the screen break

**Emily Perkovich** (she/her) is from the Chicago-land area. She is the Editor in Chief of Querencia Press, a poetry reader with Split Lip Mag, and on the Women in Leadership Advisory Board with Valparaiso University. Her work strives to erase the stigma surrounding trauma victims and their responses. She is a Best of the Net nominee, a SAFTA scholarship recipient, and is previously published with *Harness Magazine, Rogue Agent, Coffin Bell Journal,* and *Awakenings* among others. She is the author of the poetry collections *Godshots Wanted: Apply Within* (Sunday Mornings at the River), *The Number 12 Looks Just Like You* (Finishing Line Press), *baby, sweetheart, honey* (Alien Buddha Press), & *Manipulate Me, Babe—I Trust You* (GutSlut Press) as well as the novella *Swallow.* You can find her on IG @undermeyou or Twitter @emily_perkovich

www.ingramcontent.com/pod-product-compliance
Lightning Source LLC
Chambersburg PA
CBHW022110080426
42734CB00009B/1550